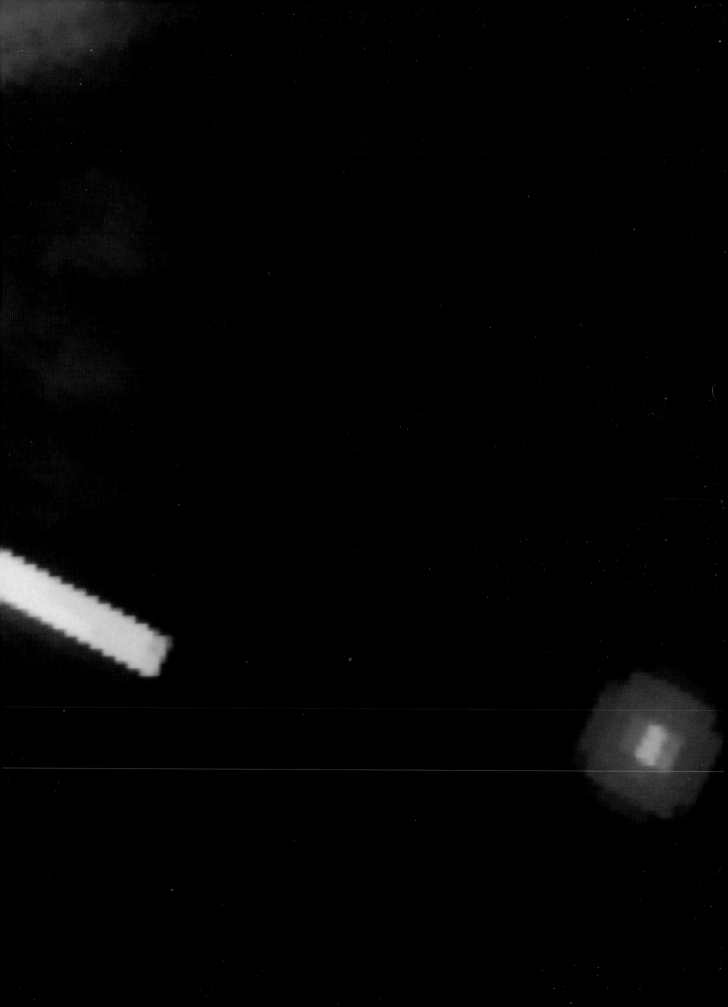

21st-century SCIENCE

SPACE

Present knowledge • Future trends

Written by Robin Kerrod

A+

Smart Apple Media

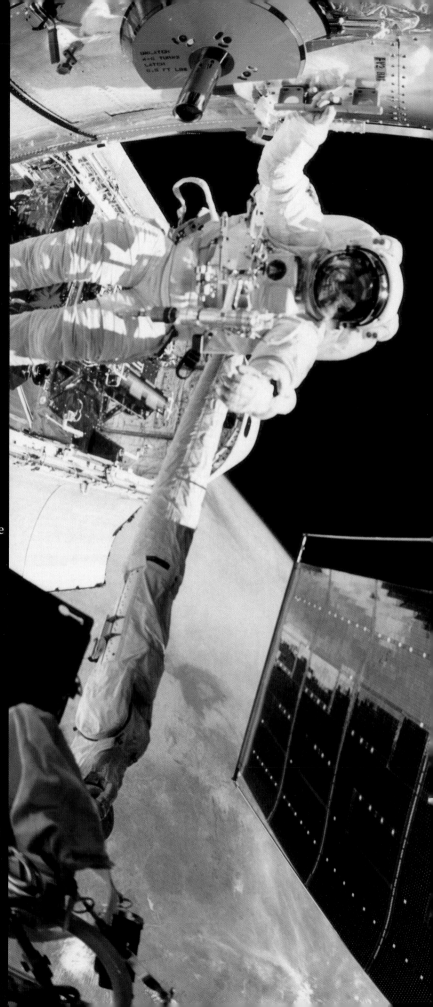

First published in 2002 by
Franklin Watts
96 Leonard Street
London EC2A 4XD

Franklin Watts Australia
45-51 Huntley Street
Alexandria
NSW 2015

Editors Penny Clarke/Constance Novis
Design Billin Design Solutions
Editor in Chief John C. Miles
Art Director Jonathan Hair

Printed in the United States of America

Picture Credits
Robin Kerod: 21b, 23
NASA: 6–7, 18, 24, 36, 37
Spacecharts: end papers, 4–5, 8, 9 © the
Association of Universities for Research in
Astronomy Inc., 10, 11 NASA, 12–13, 13t E.
Karkoschka (University of Arizona) & NASA,
4, 15t, 16, 17, 19, 20t NASA, 22, 25t, 26–27,
28–29, 30–31, 32 NASA, 33 NASA, 34 NASA,
35 NASA, 38 NASA, 39 NASA, 40 NASA, 41
NASA

Published in the United States by
Smart Apple Media
1980 Lookout Drive
North Mankato, Minnesota 56003

Library of Congress Cataloging-in
Publication Data

Kerrod, Robin.
Space / by Robin Kerrod.
p. cm. — (21st-century science)
Includes index.
Summary: Describes the history and
development of space stations and the
exploration of our solar system, as well as
the possibility of some day settling on the
moon and traveling to Mars.
ISBN 1-58340-351-5
1. Outer space—Juvenile literature. 2. Outer
space—Exploration—Juvenile literature.
[1. Outer space. 2 Outer space—
Exploration.] I. Title. II. 21st-century science
(Mankato, Minn.)
QB500.22.K47 2003
919.904—dc21
2003041515

First Edition

9 8 7 6 5 4 3 2 1

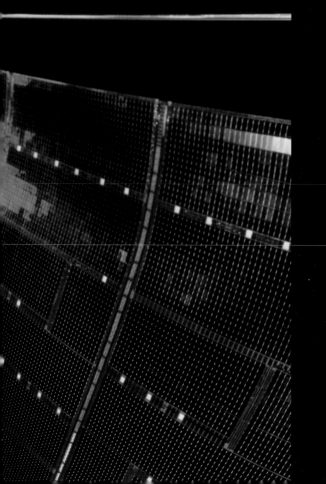

Contents

INTRODUCTION

When you look into the inky blackness of the night sky, you are looking deep into space, deep into the universe. To our early ancestors, this universe—populated by fixed stars and wandering stars (planets), broom stars (comets), and falling stars (meteors)—was profoundly mysterious, and to be feared.

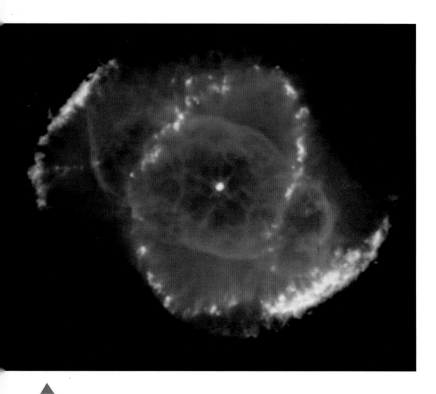

▲

Cat's eye nebula, marking the death throes of a star such as the sun.

▶▶

Billions of stars and clouds of glowing gas light up the heavens.

The starry heavens were first observed methodically around 5,000 years ago by the learned priests of the early civilizations in the Middle East, such as Babylon and Egypt. Their main purpose was to look for good or bad omens (signs) that might mean good times or bad ones. They believed that what happened in the heavens somehow affected human lives. This belief, astrology, held sway for thousands of years. Today we know that it has no scientific basis.

The first astronomers

Nevertheless, the observations by those early priest-astrologers paved the way for astronomy, the true scientific study of the heavens. Modern astronomy began with the works of the Polish cleric-physician Nicholas Copernicus (1473–1543) and the Italian scientist Galileo Galilei (1564–1642).

Copernicus figured that Earth and the other planets circle around the sun. They are part of the sun's family in space, or solar system. Until then, it was believed that all the heavenly bodies circled Earth. Galileo was one of the first people to build a telescope to study the heavens. He observed the moon and the phases of Venus and discovered four moons around the planet Jupiter.

Present knowledge

Astronomy today still depends on telescopes to investigate the secrets of the stars and space. Modern telescopes are giant-sized, with huge mirrors to gather the faint light from the heavenly bodies. Radio telescopes are used to pick up the radio waves that stars and galaxies give out. And telescopes are sent into space on satellites to see the universe more clearly and to pick up rays that we cannot detect on Earth.

Satellites spearheaded our attack on space, often called the "final frontier." The Space Age began on October 4, 1957, when Russia's *Sputnik 1* went into orbit around Earth. Cosmonaut Yuri Gagarin led the human conquest of space when he blasted into orbit on April 12, 1961.

The way ahead

Since the 1960s, space flight has become almost routine. The reusable space shuttle has been introduced, space stations have been built in orbit, and human footprints have been left on the moon. The 21st century will see humans return to the moon, this time to set up permanent bases. And astronauts will take the next "giant leap for mankind" and set out to explore Mars, known as the Red Planet.

SUN moon
AND EARTH

The sun dominates our corner of space. It is our local star, much the same as all the other stars in the night sky, but very much closer. It lies only about 93 million miles (150 million km) away—millions of times closer than most other stars.

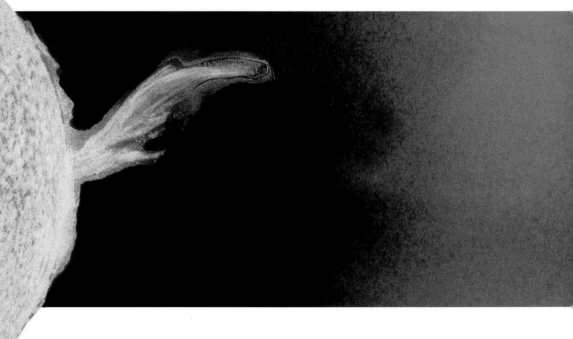

▲ *Flaming gas erupts from the boiling surface of the sun.*

Like all stars, the sun pours enormous energy into space, mainly as light and heat. This energy makes Earth a good home for millions of species (kinds) of living things, from microscopic plants to huge whales.

Scientists are now looking to the sun to play a more active part in producing power for us. Existing sources of fuel, such as oil and gas, will run out one day. But the energy the sun pours down on Earth—solar energy—will never run out. Solar energy is already being used: solar cells make electricity for spacecraft, and solar power stations generate electricity by concentrating the sun's heat with huge mirrors.

Day by day

We see the sun arc across the sky during the day. It seems to circle around Earth. But it doesn't. The sun's motion across the sky happens because Earth spins around in space every day. It also circles around the sun every 365.25 days—in other words, once a year.

The earth is made up of layers. Under a layer of air (the atmosphere) is a thin, hard layer of rocks (the crust). This rests on a thicker layer of heavier rock (the mantle). And in the middle is a great ball of molten iron and nickel (the core).

Sections (plates) of the earth's crust also move. This causes the continents to drift, which makes volcanoes erupt and creates earthquakes. The action of the weather and flowing water slowly erodes (wears away) the land, so even the highest mountains become gentle hills in the end.

The moon

Just as the sun dominates Earth's sky by day, the moon dominates it by night. Earth's only satellite, the moon travels around Earth once a month, changing its appearance as it does so as more or less of its surface is lit up by the sun.

The moon is only about a quarter as big across as Earth. Because it is much smaller, it has less gravity, or pull, but the amount of gravity is enough to cause the tides in Earth's oceans, by tugging at the waters.

Airless and barren, the moon is the only body in space that humans have reached. Between 1969 and 1972, 12 men walked on its surface.

The rugged, cratered surface of the moon's Ocean of Storms.

the PLANETS

On many nights of the year a bright star appears in the western sky just after sunset. It appears long before the other stars and is much brighter. It is sometimes called the "Evening Star." But it isn't a star at all—it is a neighboring planet, Venus. Planets are bodies that circle in orbit around the sun, like Earth does.

Venus is one of five planets that we can see in the sky with the naked eye. The others are Mercury, Mars, Jupiter, and Saturn. In addition, there are three more planets so far away that we can see them only through telescopes. With Earth, this makes nine planets.

The planets fall into two main groups. There is an inner group of four small planets—Mercury, Venus, Earth, and Mars—which lie relatively close together. Made up of rock, they are called the terrestrial, or Earth-like, planets. The planets Jupiter, Uranus, Saturn, and Neptune form a widely separated outer group. These four planets are giant-sized and are made up mainly of gas and liquid gas, mostly hydrogen. The outermost planet, Pluto, is a tiny ice ball, smaller even than our moon.

Other family members

Many other kinds of bodies belong to our solar system. Most of the planets have moons circling around them; the four giant planets alone have more than 60.

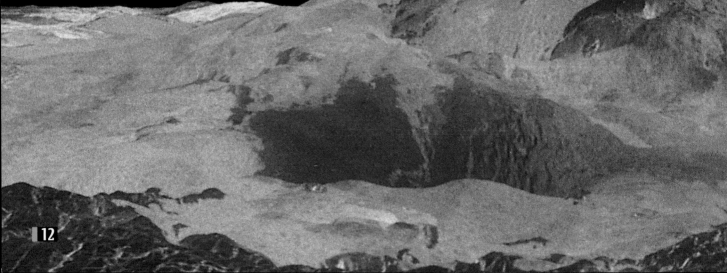

▼

Maat Mons, one of the imposing volcanoes found on our nearest planetary neighbor, Venus.

A swarm of asteroids (mini-planets) circles the sun in a band. A few come dangerously close to Earth. Spacewatch, at the University of Arizona, is one of several groups that track these near-Earth objects (NEOs) in case any are on a collision course with Earth.

Other solar systems

The sun is not the only star that has planets circling around it. Astronomers have detected extrasolar planets—planets circling around other nearby stars. To find them, astrono-mers look for stars that wobble slightly, because the pull of a planet's gravity can make a star wobble.

The first planets detected by the wobble technique were found in 1995. Since then dozens have been discovered around stars such as the sun. Most appear to be the size of Jupiter or bigger. But these stars may well have smaller, undetected planets—there may even be some similar to Earth.

Storms rage in the atmosphere of the beautiful ringed planet Saturn.

Planet Data

Planet	Av distance from sun million miles (km)	Diameter at equator miles (km)	Circles sun in
Mercury	36 (58)	3,032 (4,880)	88 days
Venus	67 (108)	7,521 (12,104)	225 days
Earth	93 (150)	7,926 (12,756)	365.25 days
Mars	142 (228)	4,220 (6,792)	687 days
Jupiter	483 (778)	88,850 (143,048)	11.9 years
Saturn	888 (1,429)	74,900 (120,540)	29.4 years
Uranus	1,787 (2,875)	31,760 (51,120)	83.7 years
Neptune	2,799 (4,505)	30,780 (49,530)	163.7 years
Pluto	3,676 (5,916)	1,430 (2,300)	248 years

the stars

On a clear night, without binoculars or a telescope, you could probably count more than 2,000 stars in the sky. With binoculars and a telescope, you could see many thousands more too faint to be seen by the naked eye.

Many stars seem to form groups, or constellations, in the sky. Ancient astronomers named them after the figures they thought they formed. And a few are well named, including Leo (lion) and Scorpius (scorpion).

Profiling the stars

Like the sun, stars are balls of white-hot gas that give off energy as light, heat, and other radiation. Stars vary in size. Supergiant stars are hundreds of millions of miles in diameter, while neutron stars are not much bigger across than an average city.

Stars look tiny because they are so far away. The light from the closest, Proxima Centauri, takes more than four years to reach Earth. Astronomers say it lies more than four light-years away.

Life and death

Like living things, stars are born, live, and then die. They are born in nebulae, great clouds of gas and dust in space. Gravity makes part of a cloud collapse, creating an ever denser ball. The temperature of the ball increases until nuclear reactions occur inside it. Then the ball begins shining as a new star.

How long a star lives and how it dies depends on its size. A star such as the sun shines for about 10 billion years before starting to die. It first expands into a huge red giant, then slowly shrinks to a tiny white dwarf.

Bigger stars have shorter lives. When they die, they swell into supergiants. Then they explode as supernovas and blast themselves apart. The star's core collapses and is crushed. It may form a neutron star so dense that a pinhead of it would weigh millions of tons. Or the core may disappear, leaving a region of intense gravity—a black hole from which not even light can escape. Astronomers believe that black holes power highly energetic galaxies.

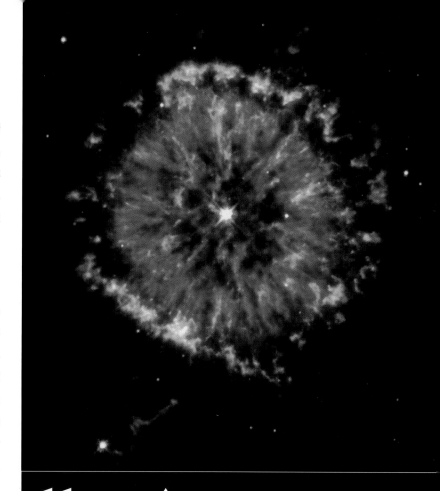

◄ ◄
The star Capella in the constellation Auriga.

▲
A huge bubble of gas surrounds a tiny white dwarf.

Life cycle of a star

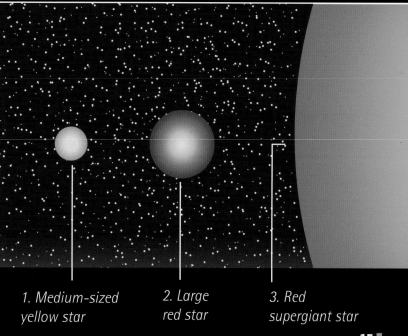

1. Medium-sized yellow star

2. Large red star

3. Red supergiant star

the GALAXIES

Wherever you look in the night sky, you see stars scattered about in the blackness that is space. So you might imagine that this is what our universe is like—stars scattered about in space. But it is not.

▲

The famous Andromeda galaxy, a spiral like ours, but much bigger.

From a great distance in space, you would see that all the stars in the sky belong to a great "star island." You would also see other star islands with empty space in between. These star islands are called galaxies.

Our galaxy is called the Milky Way. It is a huge disc of stars, with a bulge in the middle. The stars are gathered mainly on long arms that curve out from the central bulge. Galaxies that have this shape are called spirals. Others, known as ellipticals, have no arms and are oval in shape. Still others, called irregulars, have no particular shape.

Our galaxy contains at least 100 billion stars. It is so big that a beam of light would take 100,000 years to cross from one side to the other. So, it is 100,000 light-years across.

Galactic neighbors

Our galaxy does not travel alone through space. It travels with about 30 other galaxies, which together form what is called the Local Group. Only three of our galactic neighbors are visible to the naked eye.

In Australia and South America, you can see two of them as misty patches, called the Large and Small Magellanic Clouds (LMC and SMC). The LMC is the closest galaxy to us, about 170,000 light-years away, but it is only about one-third the size of our own galaxy.

A much larger galaxy is found in the constellation Andromeda, in northern skies, again seen as a misty patch. This galaxy is about half as big as our own and lies an amazing 2.3 million light-years away.

Active galaxies

Most galaxies give out the amount of energy we would expect from a collection of billions of stars. But a few give off exceptional energy, and it is these galaxies that have been the subject of intense investigation in recent years. Astronomers call them active galaxies. They believe that these galaxies must all be powered by black holes, those invisible relics of stellar explosions.

Some active galaxies give out their exceptional energy not as light, but as radio waves, and are known as radio galaxies. The radio galaxy Cygnus A gives off 10 million times the radio energy of an ordinary galaxy.

Another type of active galaxy is called a quasar. Quasars look like stars in our telescopes, but prove to be incredibly distant—billions of light-years away. To be visible from such a distance, they must be as bright as hundreds of galaxies put together.

▼

This active galaxy, known as Centaurus A, is one of the most powerful sources of radio waves in the heavens.

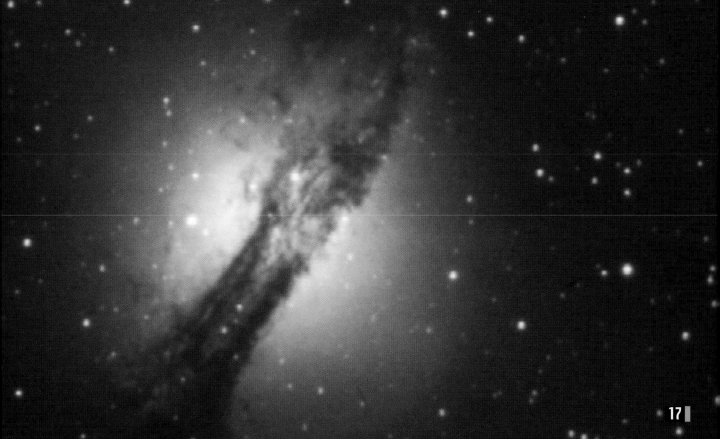

The Local Group of galaxies, which includes our own Milky Way, is just one of many clusters of galaxies found in space. Most clusters are much bigger. There is a cluster in the constellation Virgo and neighboring Coma Berenices which contains at least 3,000 galaxies.

The UNIVERSE

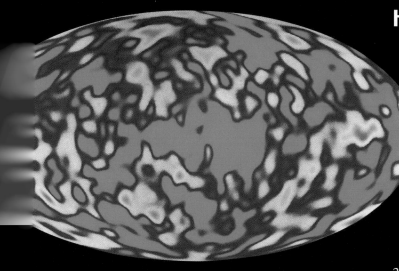

...age of
...ound space
...n supports
...Bang

How did it all begin?

Early last century, when astronomers first had giant telescopes, they discovered that almost all of the galaxies are rushing away from us and from one another. It is almost as if they had been produced in an explosion long ago, which had blasted something apart.

In fact, this is more or less what astronomers now think happened. They believe that an explosion they call the "Big Bang" took place about 15 billion years ago. This event actually created the universe of space and everything in it. It also set the universe expanding, and this is still happening today.

In the beginning, the universe was very tiny, very hot, and filled only with radiation. But, when it was only a few seconds old, it had cooled enough for atomic particles to form

In turn, the Virgo-Coma cluster forms part of a much larger supercluster.

Millions of such superclusters make up the universe. The latest observations suggest that the galaxies in the superclusters are arranged in curved sheets around vast, empty regions known as voids. On the largest scale, the voids seem to be connected, giving the universe a kind of spongy structure.

It took hundreds of thousands of years before these particles (neutrons, protons, and electrons) combined to form atoms, and billions more years for these atoms to be transformed into stars and galaxies.

How will it end?

Astronomers now think they have a clear idea of how the universe began, but they are far from sure about how it might end or indeed whether it will end. It all seems to depend on the total mass of the universe.

If the mass of the universe is large enough, the gravity, or pull, of this mass could be enough eventually to rein in the galaxies. Then the universe would stop expanding. Indeed, gravity might then pull at the galaxies and make the universe start to shrink. It might even shrink until all of its matter became crushed to nothing, in a so-called "Big Crunch."

On the other hand, if there isn't enough mass in the universe, the galaxies will continue in their headlong flight, and the universe will expand forever, or at least until it runs out of energy.

Astronomers find it difficult to measure, or even guess how massive the universe is. They can readily estimate the mass of the stars and galaxies they can see—the visible matter. But there is much matter in the universe that they can't see—called dark matter. No one knows how much dark matter there is. But there are indications that there isn't enough matter in the universe, and it will probably continue expanding.

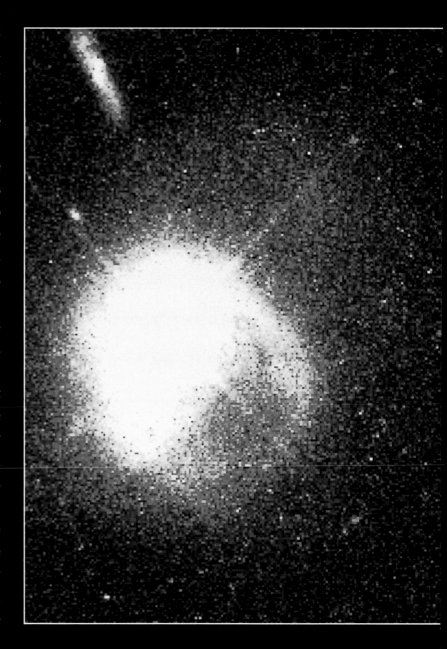

▼ *Quasars are among the most distant objects in the universe.*

LIFE in SPACE

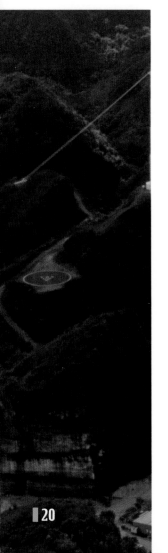

As far as we know, Earth is the only place in the universe where there is life. No traces of life have been found on any other planet in our solar system or among the stars—yet.

Of the other planets, Earth's neighbor Mars is the most likely place where life might exist. But space probes have found that conditions on Mars could not support even primitive life. It is very cold, with no oxygen to breathe. But water, which is essential to life as we know it, is present on Mars as ice at the poles. And there is water vapor in the thin atmosphere, in the form of mist and clouds. Photos taken by probes show channels on the surface, probably made by rivers, suggesting that Mars once had a milder and wetter climate. Some kind of life may have developed in this environment.

In the oceans

A major problem with guessing whether there is extraterrestrial life (life outside Earth) is that we don't know how life begins. The accepted view is that life on Earth began in a chemical "soup" in the oceans. The simple organic (carbon) compounds in this soup were produced by chemical reactions in the atmosphere, triggered by the energy in lightning.

But some astronomers argue that the organic compounds in the "soup" could have been carried to Earth by comets. The *Giotto* probe detected traces of organic compounds in

Halley's Comet in 1986. Astronomers hope to have more evidence of these compounds when the probe *Stardust* returns to Earth in 2006 with samples from Comet Wild 2.

Searching for ET

Radio astronomers have found that simple, organic compounds are common in space, for example, in glowing nebulae. So, perhaps life too is common in space. There are billions of stars like the sun, and probably millions of planets like Earth, with the right conditions for life, and probably intelligent life.

So why haven't we heard from any extraterrestrials (ETs)? It's the distance—radio signals between us might take thousands of years. Even so, the search for extraterrestrial intelligence, called SETI, is on. One project uses the giant radio telescope at Arecibo, Puerto Rico, in the Caribbean. Home computer users can help through SETI@home—letting their computers process incoming signals when idle.

◄ ◄

Mist in the canyons of Mars. Did life once exist there?

▼

The Arecibo radio telescope, on Puerto Rico—searching for life in space.

new
EYES
and EARS

In 1609, Galileo made his first telescope using a combination of glass lenses to gather and focus the light from the stars. This type of telescope is called a refractor, because lenses refract, or bend, light.

Around 1672, Isaac Newton built a different type of telescope that used mirrors to gather and focus light. This type is called a reflector, because mirrors reflect light.

Today, all big astronomical telescopes are reflectors. Big reflectors are easier to build than big refractors because it is easier to support a big mirror than a big lens. The first giant reflector, the Hale, was built at the Mount Palomar Observatory near Los Angeles in 1948. Its light-gathering mirror is more than 200 inches (5 m) across.

Some of the latest telescopes have mirrors double this size. But the mirrors are made up of many segments, each individually supported. They are controlled by computers and aligned so that they always form a mirror of the most perfect shape. This technique is known as active optics.

◄ *The Effelsberg radio telescope, near Bonn, Germany.*

The twin Keck telescopes at Mauna Kea Observatory, in Hawaii, are telescopes of this type and can work in unison to produce superlative images of the heavens. Each has a mirror 33 feet (10 m) across, made up of 36 segments. At the European Southern Observatory in Chile, four identical telescopes have been built with mirrors 26 feet (8 m) in diameter. Used together, they form the Very Large Telescope (VLT) and produce images nearly as good as those that the Hubble Space Telescope sends back.

On the radio

Astronomers also study the radio waves from stars. To do this, they use radio telescopes, which are nothing like ordinary telescopes. They are usually huge, metal dishes, which reflect incoming signals onto a central antenna. Circuits amplify the signals and feed them to a receiver. Then they are fed into a computer to produce false-color radio "images."

Currently, the most powerful radio telescope is the Very Large Array at Socorro, New Mexico. It consists of 27 movable dishes, each 82 feet (25 m) across. Mounted on rails, they can be moved into various configurations. Used together, they have a receiving area equivalent to a dish 17 miles (27 km) across.

Even bigger dishes are created by linking together radio telescopes from different observatories. This technique, called Very Long Baseline Interferometry (VLBI), could create "dishes" the size of Earth—or even bigger if radio telescope satellites were used.

▼
Observatory domes at Kitt Peak National Observatory near Tucson, Arizona.

TELESCOPES in SPACE

Even when they use the latest giant telescopes, astronomers at observatories cannot get a perfect view of stars and space. This is because they have to peer through Earth's atmosphere.

To them, the atmosphere is a dirty window looking out into space. It is full of dust and drops of moisture, and is constantly moving. This means it tends to blur the light coming in. To overcome this problem, astronomers are now sending their telescopes, and other instruments, into space on satellites. There, far above Earth's atmosphere, astronomers can view the heavens clearly.

Hubble's telescope

Best known of all the astronomy satellites that have been launched is the Hubble Space Telescope (HST). It was named after Edwin Hubble, who pioneered study of the galaxies during the early 1900s. The HST is a reflector, using a light-gathering mirror 7.9 feet (2.4 m) across. It views stars and space with amazing clarity and, since its launch in 1990, has been sending back incredible pictures of stellar

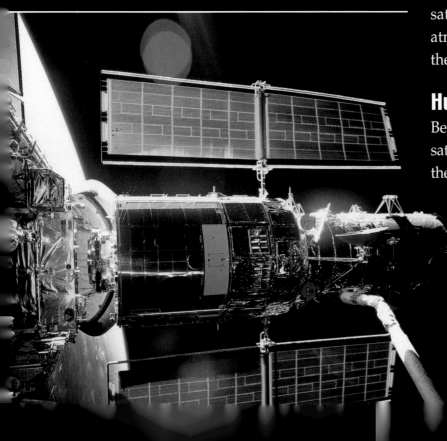

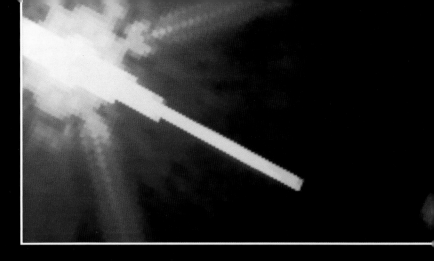

nurseries, exploding stars, super-brilliant quasars, and places where black holes seem to lurk.

Seeing the invisible

The Hubble telescope looks at the universe in ordinary light, just like telescopes do on the ground. But light is only one of the ways in which stars give off their energy. They also give off other kinds of rays, or radiation, which we can't see with our eyes. These invisible rays belong to the same family of rays as light—they are part of a family of electromagnetic waves. They include gamma rays, X-rays, ultraviolet rays, microwaves, and radio waves.

To get the complete story about what stars are like, astronomers really need to study these rays as well. They can study radio waves with radio telescopes (page 23) because radio waves pass unchanged through the atmosphere. But the other invisible rays from space are blocked or absorbed by the atmosphere. So astronomers have to study these rays using astronomy satellites. By computer-processing the signals they receive, satellites can produce images of what the stars and galaxies would look like if our eyes could detect the invisible rays. Often these images show quite a different picture of the heavens than we see in ordinary light.

New windows

Astronomy satellites open up totally new windows on space. X-ray satellites, such as the Chandra Observatory, spot mysterious X-ray bursters that for an instant outshine every other object in the sky. Infrared satellites, such as IRAS, with instruments cooled by liquid helium nearly to absolute zero, detect feebly glowing bodies. Microwave satellites, such as COBE, observe the general background radiation of the universe and find evidence of the Big Bang that created the universe in the first place. Ultraviolet satellites, such as XMM-Newton, spot the presence of hot, young stars.

The Hubble Space Telescope captures spectacular images of giant and dwarf stars.

◄ ◄

The Hubble Space Telescope is regularly recovered and repaired in orbit by astronauts from the space shuttle.

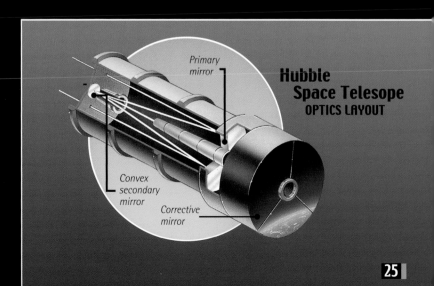

Primary mirror

Convex secondary mirror

Corrective mirror

Hubble Space Telesope
OPTICS LAYOUT

DEEP SPACE PROBES

In February 2001, a tiny spacecraft named *NEAR-Shoemaker* made a gentle touchdown on a remote asteroid named Eros. It had set off from Earth five years before and had travelled more than two billion miles (3 billion km) to its target. It was an amazing feat of navigation by space scientists at NASA's Jet Propulsion Laboratory (JPL) near Los Angeles.

Deep-space explorers are known as probes. They take the astronomer's instruments and cameras to places humans can't reach—yet. Probes have now explored all the planets except Pluto. And what wonders they have revealed: for example, that Mercury is baking hot and heavily pitted with craters; that Venus is even hotter and shaped by volcanoes; and that Mars once had running water.

The problems

Navigating a space probe for years and across billions of miles of space to a moving target is difficult to say the least. First, the probe must be launched from Earth at exactly the right speed. The minimum speed it needs to escape from Earth's gravity is 25,000 miles (40,000 km) per hour, a speed which is known as the escape velocity. Secondly, the probe must be launched in exactly the right direction. A few degrees off at launch, and the probe could miss its target by millions of miles.

Powerful computers plot an accurate course, or trajectory, for the probe, allowing for the effects of gravity on it throughout its journey from Earth, the sun, and other planets. Sometimes the gravity of the planets is used deliberately to increase the speed of the probe and change its direction. It was this technique, called gravity assist, that enabled *Voyager 2* to visit four planets in the 1970s and 1980s.

Another major problem is the time lag in communications. Even though radio signals travel at the speed of light, they can take hours to travel between Earth and a distant probe. So any instructions to the probe from ground controllers must be sent well in advance. And for critical maneuvers, such as landing on an asteroid, a probe must rely on its own brain, its computer.

Winging their way

Space probes may carry out their exploration in several ways. Some explore their target as they fly by.

That is what *Pioneer 10* did when it encountered Jupiter in 1974. JPL controllers are still in communication with it, even though it is now more than seven billion miles (11 billion km) from Earth. The two-way time lag to the probe is now 22 hours!

Some probes may orbit their target, such as *Magellan*, which mapped Venus using radar beams in the 1990s. Some may land on their target. Several landers have set down on Mars. One (*Pathfinder*, 1997) carried a rover named *Sojourner*, which analyzed nearby rocks. Further rovers will be exploring Mars in the years to come, followed by so-called sample-and-return missions to bring Martian soil back to Earth. They will probably beat another sample-and-return mission already underway—the Stardust mission to Comet Wild 2. The spacecraft should catch some comet dust in 2004 and bring it back to Earth in 2006.

◄ ◄

An artist's impression of the Huygens *probe descending to the surface of Saturn's moon Titan in 2004.*

▲

Space probe Magellan, *which used radar to map Venus from orbit in the 1990s.*

SATELLITES AND ROCKETS

Earth exerts a powerful force—gravity—on everything on or near it. It is gravity that keeps our feet on the ground and the water in the oceans. To launch objects into space, we must somehow overcome gravity. How do we do it? The simple answer is speed. If we launch something into the air with the right speed and in the right direction, it will go up and up and start circling Earth. It will become a satellite.

We must propel an object to a colossal speed to create a satellite—about 17,500 miles (28,000 km) per hour. This is called the orbital velocity. Satellites may be launched into a path, or orbit, just a few hundreds of miles high, or tens of thousands. It all depends on the job they have to do. For example, communications satellites relay telephone calls and e-mails

▲

European remote-sensing satellite ERS, *pictured in orbit.*

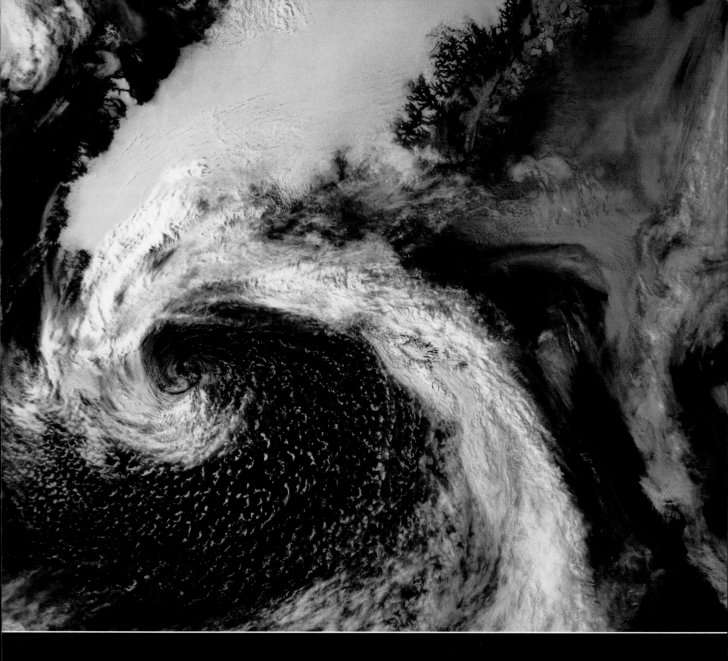

around the world from an orbit some 22,300 miles (36,000 km) high over the equator.

Rocket power

The only engine powerful enough to launch satellites into space is the rocket. It is also the only engine that can work in space because it carries oxygen to burn its fuel. Other engines, such as the jet, burn their fuel with oxygen they take in from the air.

In a rocket, the fuel and the substance that provides oxygen are called propellants. Most space rockets burn liquid propellants, such as liquid hydrogen (fuel) and liquid oxygen. The space shuttle's main engines use these propellants. However, no single rocket is powerful enough to launch a satellite.

▲

A weather satellite image showing clouds spiralling around a "low" near the British Isles.

SATELLITES and ROCKETS

One stage at a time

Several rocket units, or stages, have to be joined together to produce enough power. This arrangement is called a step rocket. Each stage fires in turn and then falls away. The rocket gets lighter and lighter, making it easier to thrust its payload (cargo) into orbit. Most space launching rockets, or launch vehicles, have three main stages. They may also have extra rockets strapped on, called boosters, to give them more power when it is needed at lift-off.

The way ahead

The kinds of rockets used today will be used in launch vehicles for some time to come. But other kinds of engines may be used to propel craft in space. One is the ion engine. This device produces only a tiny thrust (push), but it can exert this thrust for a very long time. Using power from solar cells, the engine produces a stream of electrically charged gas particles, known as ions.

◄

Nine external boosters fire as a Delta rocket lifts off, carrying a weather satellite.

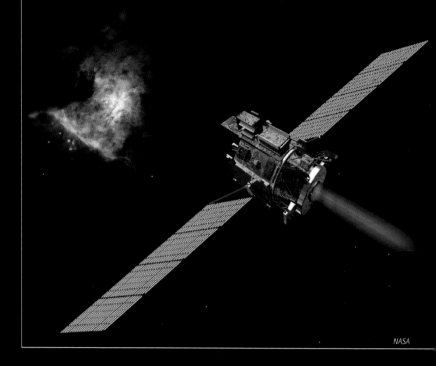

Deep Space 1, *pictured travelling through space, ion engine firing.*

Ion-engine technology was first used successfully on the probe *Deep Space 1*, launched in 1998. Powered only by an ion engine, it visited asteroid Braille in 1999 and flew through Comet Borrelly in 2001, taking the first clear pictures of a comet nucleus (center).

Experimental nuclear rocket engines have also been tested. They may hold the key for further manned exploration of the solar system, for example, to Mars, the Red Planet. They would use the energy produced in a compact nuclear reactor to propel streams of hydrogen gas.

Launching a satellite into orbit

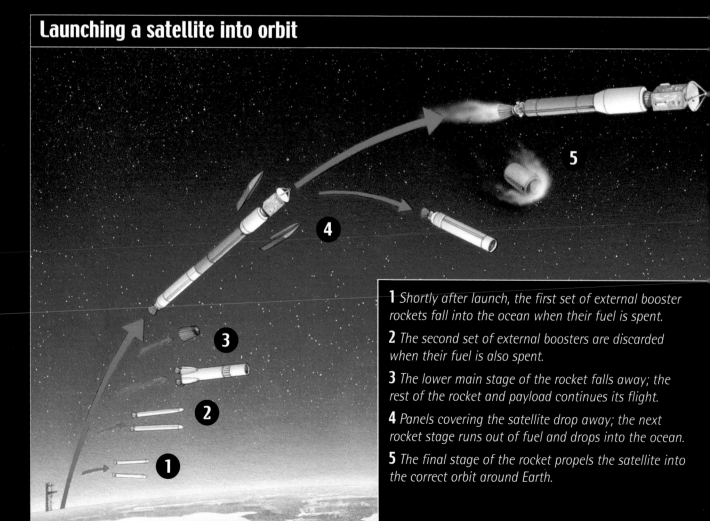

1 *Shortly after launch, the first set of external booster rockets fall into the ocean when their fuel is spent.*

2 *The second set of external boosters are discarded when their fuel is also spent.*

3 *The lower main stage of the rocket falls away; the rest of the rocket and payload continues its flight.*

4 *Panels covering the satellite drop away; the next rocket stage runs out of fuel and drops into the ocean.*

5 *The final stage of the rocket propels the satellite into the correct orbit around Earth.*

SPACE planes

The ordinary rocket launch vehicles used to launch satellites can be used only once—they are expendable. Using them once is a great waste of expensive hardware. This is one reason U.S. space scientists developed the space shuttle. It is a space launch system that uses the same equipment time and time again.

The first shuttle flight took place on April 12, 1981, 20 years to the day after Yuri Gagarin pioneered human space travel. Now there is a shuttle flight every few weeks. Russia also built a space shuttle, named *Buran*, but it made only one flight, in 1988. Russian cosmonauts still travel into space in expendable Soyuz spacecraft, first introduced in 1967.

Shuttle hardware

The shuttle system has three main parts—orbiter, external tank, and solid-rocket boosters (SRBs). Of these, only the external tank is wasted.

The winged orbiter is about 120 feet (37 m) long with a wingspan of nearly 79 feet (24 m). It takes off vertically like a rocket, mounted on the external tank that holds fuel for its three main engines. They fire at lift-off, together with the SRBs strapped to the tank. Two minutes later, the SRBs separate and parachute back to Earth. After about six more minutes, the external tank is empty and is jettisoned.

The orbiter continues into orbit. After its mission is over, it fires retrorockets to slow it so that it succumbs to the pull of gravity. As the orbiter re-enters the atmosphere, air resistance slows it more. It then glides down to land on the runway.

The Kennedy Space Center in Florida is the base for space shuttle operations. Shuttles take off and usually land there. Four orbiters make up the shuttle fleet—*Columbia*, *Discovery*, *Atlantis*, and *Endeavor*. *Endeavor* was a replacement craft for *Challenger*, an orbiter that exploded just after its launch in 1986.

SSTO

The shuttle system works well and has proved generally reliable, but it is still based on old technology. The future seems to be with what are termed single-stage-to-orbit (SSTO) vehicles. These, unlike current launchers, have hybrid air-breathing jet/rocket engines, or scramjets.

While in the atmosphere, they use the oxygen there to burn their fuel. In space, they use on-board oxygen.

SSTO technologies are being tested in the NASA-sponsored X-33 vehicle. This delta-winged craft is like the X-38 crew-return vehicle, developed to return crews from the International Space Station.

Other nations have similar projects. India's Avatar space-plane is one. At first powered by a turbofan, it switches first to a scramjet and then to a rocket in airless space.

◄ ◄

All rockets firing, space shuttle Endeavor *thunders off the launch pad.*

◄

Returning from space, Endeavor *lands on a runway, braked by parachutes.*

33

LIVING in SPACE

To get an idea of what it's like to live in space, imagine you are an astronaut taking a trip into orbit on a space shuttle. When you blast off the launch pad, rockets hurtle you into space with enormous acceleration. From rest, you reach a speed of 17,500 miles (28,000 km) per hour in less than 10 minutes.

▲

Mealtimes on Earth are not like this! Spilled drinks form round blobs in zero-G.

This exposes your body to forces up to four times the pull of gravity, or 4Gs. Yet once you're in orbit, all these forces seem to disappear, and you become weightless.

Weightlessness, or zero-G, affects all your life in orbit. You can't walk around in your spacecraft because if you press your feet down on the floor, you just bounce up. When you bend down to pick something up, you begin turning somersaults. In any case, there is no "down" or "up"

in space because with no apparent gravity, nothing falls. It just floats about—and so do you.

Life in zero-G

Day-to-day living in weightless conditions takes some getting used to. You move by pulling and pushing yourself around. If you want to stay put to eat a meal, say, you must anchor your feet and stick down trays, cutlery, and food containers, otherwise they'll float away.

Avoid crumbly foods because the crumbs will escape into the air and perhaps get into equipment. Many space foods are dehydrated and must be mixed with water before being eaten. You can't pour something to drink with your meals because liquids won't pour in space. You must suck them up with a straw.

Life-support

Food and water form part of what is called life-support—things to keep you alive in space. All food must be taken with you, but water is produced by the fuel cells that provide the spacecraft with electrical power. They make water chemically by combining hydrogen and oxygen gases. There is usually plenty of water on a spacecraft, not only for drinking but also for washing and, on space stations, even for a shower.

"Running" water on spacecraft is made to run with the help of a stream of air. Air streams are also used to flush space lavatories. The air sucks body wastes into storage compartments. Space lavatories look similar to toilets on Earth. But they have some notable extra features, such as foot straps and a seat belt! A hose removes urine.

Another essential life-support feature is air conditioning. Oxygen must be supplied for breathing, and the carbon dioxide that is exhaled

must be removed, along with odors. Temperature and humidity are controlled to give a comfortable "shirt-sleeves" environment.

Going walkabout

Work in space may include extra-vehicular activity (EVA), or space-walking. For EVA you need a space-suit. This has its own life-support system, providing oxygen to breathe and insulation from radiation and the temperature extremes of space: up to 248 °F (120 °C) in the sun and down to -238 °F (-150 °C) in the shade. You leave and re-enter the spacecraft through an airlock, a small chamber that can be pressurized and depressurized.

▲

Spacewalking astronauts grapple with a huge communications satellite that needs to be repaired.

space MEDICINE

Human bodies are designed for, and are accustomed to, living on the surface of the earth, where there is air to breathe, comfortable temperatures, and the ordinary 1G pull of gravity.

Until cosmonaut Yuri Gagarin went into space in 1961, no one knew for certain whether the body could withstand the rigors of space flight.

We now know that the human body can cope with the stresses and dangers of space flight without being harmed. Hundreds of astronauts and cosmonauts have journeyed into space, a few for more than a year.

Russian cosmonaut Valery Polyakov holds the space duration record with a flight in 1994–95 of nearly 438 days.

Effects on the body

In the short term, however, weightlessness does affect the body in several ways. The study of these effects is known as space medicine. Space seems to have four main effects on three of the body's systems. The first system to be affected is the balance organs in the ear, known as the vestibular system. This causes more than half of all astronauts to suffer from "space sickness," or space adaptation syndrome, for the first few days of flight.

The second to be affected is the circulatory, or cardiovascular, system. And the third system to be affected is the musculo-skeletal system, the bones and muscles.

▼

Exercising regularly is important on long space missions to stop muscles from wasting away.

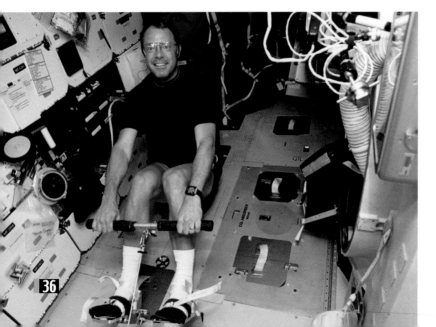

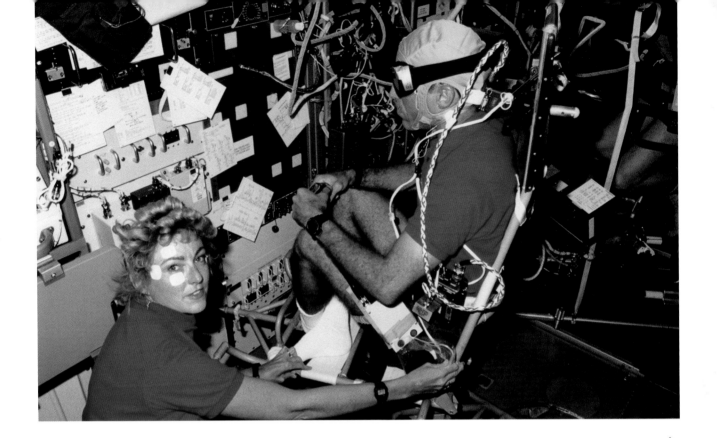

▲

Astronauts become guinea pigs for life-science experiments in orbit.

Blood and bones

Freed from gravity, the blood redistributes itself around the body, pushing more up into the head and upper torso. As a result, astronauts get a fat face and "bird legs." In zero-G, the bones in the spine expand, making astronauts up to two inches (5 cm) taller in space than they are on Earth. A more worrying effect is that there is a marked loss, or atrophy, of bone and muscle tissue, particularly in the legs. This is because the body no longer has to battle against gravity when it moves.

Back to Earth

Up in space, the zero-G effects on the body cause few problems. But they can cause trouble when astronauts return to Earth, especially after long flights. When astronauts drop down from orbit and re-enter Earth's atmosphere, they experience powerful G-forces of braking, or deceleration. This comes as a shock to a body used to zero-G. Blood tends to flow back away from the head and brain, which could cause blackouts. Therefore, returning astronauts usually wear pressure suits to restrict blood movement.

To cope with bone and muscle loss, long-term astronauts need to get regular exercise in space. They do this on specially designed treadmills or bicycles. On return to Earth, they may be a little shaky on their legs at first, but they regain their strength after a few days. It may take weeks before their body weight and bone and muscle tissue return to normal.

SPACE STATIONS

In the early days of space travel, astronauts remained in space for relatively short periods. Even the Apollo missions to the moon lasted less than two weeks. There was no time or room on the cramped spacecraft to carry out worthwhile scientific research or experiments. This led to the development of the first space stations, in which astronauts could stay in space for much longer periods.

Russia launched the first of seven Salyut space stations in 1971. Two years later, the United States launched Skylab, in which three teams of astronauts spent up to 84 days in space. They carried out a punishing work schedule and proved conclusively that humans could readily adapt to living in space without coming to any harm. Later, in Salyut 6 and 7, and then in Russia's last space station, Mir, some cosmonauts spent more than a year in space.

International Space Station

Mir was permanently manned for 15 years before it met a fiery end in Earth's atmosphere in March 2001. As Mir became history, a new space station was taking shape in orbit— the International Space Station (ISS). The U.S. and Russia are the two major partners in the ISS, along with Europe, Japan, Canada, and Italy.

The United States, through NASA, is overseeing construction and providing much of the hardware, including laboratory and habitation modules, solar power arrays, and airlock and connecting nodes. Russia is supplying service and laboratory modules. Europe, through the European Space Agency (ESA), is supplying a laboratory module, as is Japan. Canada's contribution is a robot handling facility, while Italy will provide "logistics" modules, which will carry supplies and equipment.

ISS assembly

When completed, the ISS will be the biggest structure ever to orbit Earth. More than 330 feet (100 m) long and nearly 250 feet (75 m) across, it will have a mass of more than 440 tons (400 t). It will orbit at an altitude of around 250 miles (400 km), circling Earth about every 90 minutes.

The ISS is being assembled piece by piece using U.S. space shuttles and Russian unmanned Proton rockets. Russia launched the first piece of the station, the Zarya control module, in November 1998. Two weeks later, the U.S. unit Unity was linked to it. Unity was a connecting unit, or node, to which other modules could later dock (link up).

The launch of Russia's Zvezda service module in July 2000 provided life-support facilities for manning the fledgling space station. And the first crew took up residence in November for a four-month stay. By early 2002, sets of giant solar arrays, a U.S. laboratory module (Destiny) and airlock (Quest), and a Russian docking compartment (Pirs) had been linked to the earlier units. Since then, assembly operations have continued at an equally hectic pace, aiming for completion around 2006. The ISS should have an operational life of at least 10 years, and its cost could reach $100 billion.

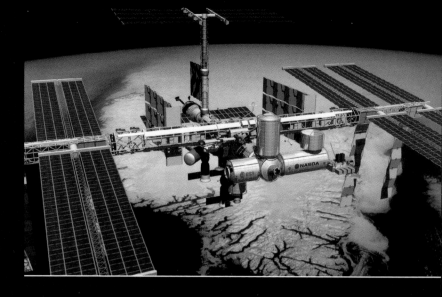

▲

Final configuration of the International Space Station, around 2006.

◄◄

Space station Mir, pictured from the space shuttle Atlantis. Space shuttles flew several missions to Mir and exchanged astronauts.

SETTING UP BASE

Apollo 17 *astronaut working at Taurus-Littrow during the last Apollo landing mission in 1972.*

The experience gained in assembling the International Space Station will lead to the construction of other space structures in the years ahead, maybe to a dedicated space-engineering complex.

The first structures space engineers might tackle could be orbiting solar power stations. They would use banks of solar cells many miles wide to capture the sun's energy, then beam it back to Earth. Such solar power satellites might become necessary later this century when the world begins to run out of fossil fuels.

Then space engineers may build spacecraft designed to travel farther into space, launching them from orbit. This requires much less power than launching them from the surface of the earth through the atmosphere.

Lunar base

First target, of course, would be the moon. Astronauts could reach the moon using techniques such as those used in the Apollo project. A lunar ferry would deliver them into lunar orbit, maybe to a space station.

From there, they would descend to the surface in a lander. No new technologies should be involved.

When humans return to the moon, they will stay there. They will build temporary shelters, maybe out of empty rocket casings. Later, they will build more permanent structures using materials manufactured from minerals they mine. Later, there may be interconnected underground complexes. Some of the domed areas could be used to grow plants for food.

Water may not be as much of a problem as was once thought because in 1998, the *Lunar Prospector* probe detected significant amounts of ice in dark craters at the lunar poles. Frozen supplies of water could be broken down to provide two other much-needed raw materials—hydrogen, for rocket fuel, and oxygen, to breathe.

Missions to Mars

The next target for human explorers has to be Mars. It is relatively close and is the only other planet humans could land on and explore safely. Years ago, many people believed that it was inhabited by Martians. But space probes have shown that Mars' atmosphere is too thin and its climate too cold to support life as we know it. There are signs, however, that the planet was once warmer and wetter than it is now.

A manned expedition to Mars would be difficult in the extreme and very expensive. The minimum time it would take for even a fleeting visit to the planet would be nearly two years. We don't yet have the technology to support such a mission. We would require far better rockets and advanced life-support systems in which everything would have to be recycled.

But such problems will eventually be overcome. Mars will be explored and conquered "because it's there," as humans continue to push back that final frontier—space.

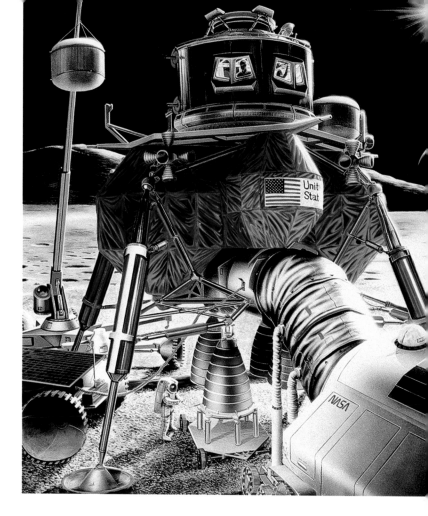

▲

At a future moon base, astronauts disembark from a lunar lander.

GLOSSARY

active galaxy
A galaxy that gives off exceptional energy.

asteroids
Small bodies that circle the sun in a huge band between Mars and Jupiter.

astronomy
The scientific study of the heavens and the heavenly bodies.

Big Bang
The theory that says the universe was created in a kind of big explosion.

black hole
A region of space with immensely strong gravity that "swallows" even light rays.

cluster
Grouping of stars or galaxies.

comet
Icy lump that shines when it nears the sun.

constellation
A grouping of stars that appear in the same direction in the sky.

crater
A pit in the surface of a planet or moon.

docking
The link-up of two spacecraft in space.

EVA
Extravehicular activity; activity outside a spacecraft, popularly called "spacewalking."

extrasolar planet
A planet circling around another star.

extraterrestrial
Not from Earth.

galaxy
A great "star island" in space.

gravity
The force that makes one bit of matter attract another.

heavens
The night sky.

launch vehicle
A multiple rocket system used to launch spacecraft.

light-year
The distance light travels in a year; used as a unit to measure distances in space.

meteor
A streak of light in the sky, produced when specks of matter from space burn up high in the air.

meteorite
A lump of matter from space that falls to the ground.

moon
Common name for a satellite of a planet.

nebula
A huge cloud of gas and dust in space.

neutron star
A tiny star made up of atomic particles called neutrons.

nuclear reactions
Reactions between the nuclei (centers) of atoms; these reactions produce the energy that makes the stars shine.

orbit
Path in space of one body around another.

planet
A large body that circles in space around the sun.

probe

A spacecraft sent to explore distant bodies, such as planets and comets.

propellants

Fuels and oxidizers (oxygen-providers) for rockets.

quasar

A very distant body that is as bright as hundreds of galaxies.

radio astronomy

The study of radio waves from space.

radio telescope

A telescope used to gather radio waves from space.

red giant

A large, dying star.

reflector

A telescope that uses mirrors to gather and focus light.

refractor

A telescope that uses lenses to gather and focus light.

rocket

A motor to power launch vehicles that carries its own supply of oxygen to burn its fuel.

satellite

A small body that orbits a larger one; in particular, an artificial, man-made object that orbits Earth.

SETI

Search for extraterrestrial intelligence; program to look for other intelligent life in space.

solar energy

The energy harnessed from the sun.

solar system

The sun's family of planets, moons, comets, asteroids, and so on.

space medicine

The study of the human body in space.

space shuttle

A reusable launch vehicle.

space station

Large, orbiting spacecraft designed for long stays in space.

spacewalking

Popular name for EVA.

star

A huge globe of intensely hot gas that gives off energy as light, heat, and other radiation.

step rocket

A system of rockets joined together, each firing in turn.

supergiant

The biggest kind of star.

supernova

The catastrophic explosion of a massive supergiant star.

terrestrial

Of or like Earth.

universe

Space and everything it contains.

weightlessness

Condition in orbiting spacecraft when gravity appears not to exist.

white dwarf

Tiny, dense star.

zero-G

Another term for weightlessness.

INDEX

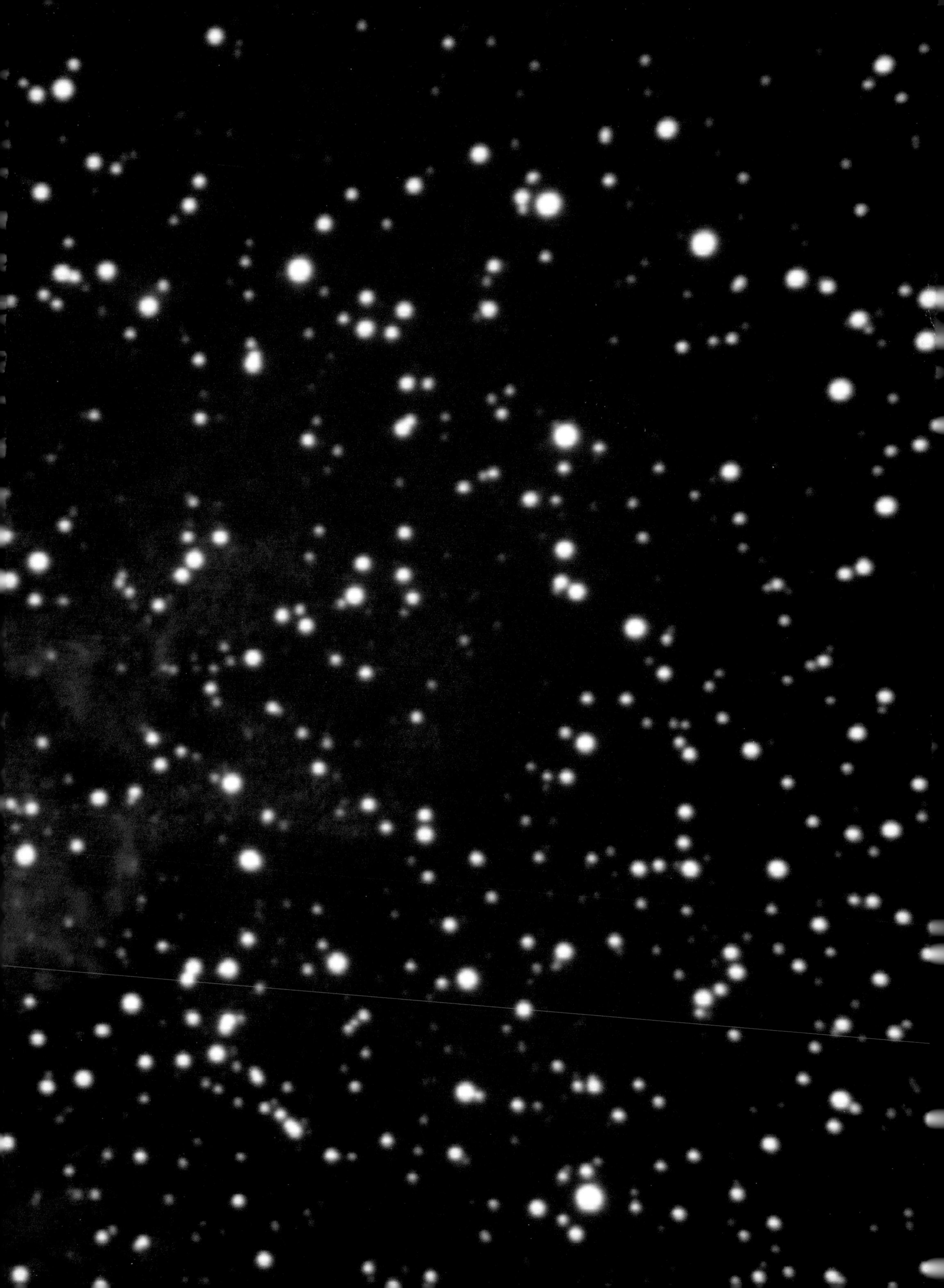